For my favorite lawyers, Jack and Julie.
—D. Robbins

To the Baders in my life: Henry and Drew.
—S. Green

All rights reserved. Published by Scholastic Press, an imprint of Scholastic Inc., *Publishers since 1920*. SCHOLASTIC, SCHOLASTIC PRESS, and associated logos are trademarks and/or registered trademarks of Scholastic Inc.

The publisher does not have any control over and does not assume any responsibility for author or third-party websites or their content.

Library of Congress Cataloging-in-Publication Data Available

ISBN 978-1-338-76766-7 (PB) / 978-1-338-76767-4 (RLB)

10 9 8 7 6 5 4 3 2 1   21 22 23 24 25

Printed in China   38

First edition, December 2021

Cover Design by Brian LaRossa
Interior Design by Jaime Lucero

YOU ARE A STAR, RUTH BADER GINSBURG

WRITTEN BY
DEAN ROBBINS

ILLUSTRATED BY
SARAH GREEN

SCHOLASTIC PRESS ★ NEW YORK

Do you know what I loved most about growing up in Brooklyn, New York?

Playing with the boys in my neighborhood.

We used to jump from one garage roof to another.

But do you know what I hated about growing up?

I was always treated differently than the boys.

People didn't think I was as smart or as strong as they were, just because I was a girl.

We'll see about that!

Adults picked on me for being left-handed.

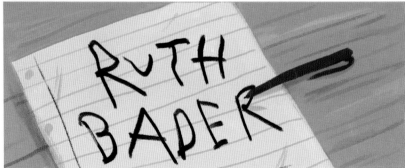

My teacher told me to use my right hand instead—which was a *really* bad idea!

DOWN WITH DISCRIMINATION!

Discrimination is when people are treated differently because of who they are, including their race, age, gender, religion, or disability. I hated discrimination more than anything! What could a small, quiet, left-handed Jewish girl from Brooklyn do to stop it?

In my neighborhood, most women stayed at home while men had jobs.

But from my trips to the library, I knew that women could do amazing things.

I read about brave female pilots and detectives.

I loved stories about the Greek goddess Athena, who charged into battle with a helmet and shield.

I wanted to charge into battle, too!

I hoped to become a singer when I grew up.

But no one else wanted me to be one!

I ♥ MY MOM

My mother, Celia Bader, was my greatest hero. She taught me to aim high and care about others. Like many women of her time, she had no chance to get a college education. But she loved learning so much that she would read books while walking through Brooklyn's crowded streets!

I worked really hard in high school.

Twirling batons.

Playing the cello.

Writing for the newspaper.

Making speeches.

I was preparing to do something great with my life, but I wasn't sure what.

Mom taught me that the best way to win an argument is by showing respect.

You know what? She was right!

THE LAND OF THE FREE

I did a school report about the Constitution, our country's most important set of laws. It lists all our freedoms, also known as rights. These rights allow us to say what we want, write what we want, and worship how we want. I learned that the Constitution has changed over time to become fairer for everyone. But if the United States wanted to make it even *better*, I had a few ideas of my own!

My parents saved money so I could go to college in 1950.

That's where I learned what lawyers do.

Lawyers know everything about our country's laws.

The best thing is, they use their knowledge to solve people's problems.

Lawyers work in a place called a court, where they meet with judges who wear long black robes.

A lawyer explains a person's problem to a judge by making an argument.

If the judge and others agree with the argument, the lawyer wins.

Problem solved!

My professor said that good lawyers could make our country a better place.

I wanted to be one of those myself.

To prove that a woman could do well in college, I needed to work as hard as I could.

So I studied in the quietest place I could find!

CARE TO DANCE?

My college classmates thought I cared only about studying. But I took time out for dancing, too. You should have seen me do a dance called the Lindy Hop. I whirled and twirled!

At college, I met the marvelous Marty Ginsburg. In some ways, Marty and I were very different.

I was short and he was tall.

I was serious and he was silly.

I was shy and he was outgoing.

But we both believed in the same things.

Equality and justice!

We wanted to spend our lives together—and even to become lawyers together.

It would give us so much to talk about in our married life.

I knew Marty admired my intelligence.

He also seemed to like my smile!

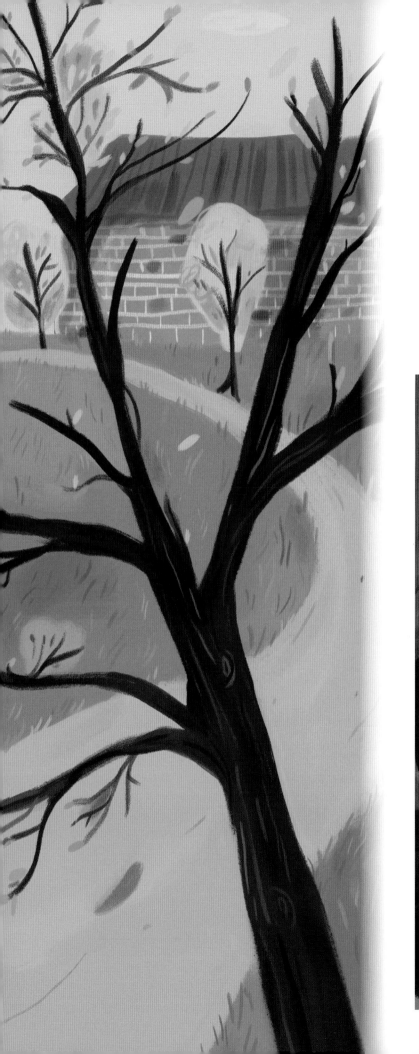

STORIES IN SONG

Marty and I liked reading, sports, and traveling. Most of all, we liked going to operas together. An opera is a story acted out onstage with singing instead of talking. I enjoyed the singers' beautiful voices—not to mention their fancy wigs!

Marty and I got married, had a baby named Jane, and started attending the same law school.

That was a lot for two young adults to handle.

So we agreed to share all the household chores equally—well, *almost* all of them.

Marty took over the cooking after I made the world's worst tuna casserole!

In my law school, the main building did not have a restroom for women.

I had to race to another building and make it back in time for class!

WOMEN KEEP OUT

Law schools did not accept many women. Would you believe that my school even banned women from the library? I wanted to prove myself by becoming the top student in my class. Make way for Ruth Bader Ginsburg!

I graduated from law school with high honors, but at first nobody would hire me.

Male lawyers did not believe that women could handle this difficult career.

When I did get a job, I set out to show how awesome we can be.

I became an expert lawyer, then a leading law professor.

By 1972, I was ready to pursue my passion.

Fighting discrimination!

If I got too serious, Marty and Jane tried to make me laugh.

Whenever I giggled, Jane wrote it down in a book!

FAMILY FIRST

Marty and I had another child, a boy named James. Even with my tiring job, I made sure to come home every night to eat and play with him and Jane. When they went to sleep, I got to work. I piled up law books on the dining room table, reading and writing until three in the morning. Want to know my secret for staying up late? Ice cream and prunes!

I got my chance with the case of Lieutenant Sharron Frontiero.

The United States military would not pay her as much as men who did the same job.

I wanted Sharron to get the money she deserved.

I also wanted to end discrimination for all women.

That meant making an argument in the country's most important court.

THE SUPREME COURT!

The huge building in Washington, DC, had tall columns, marble floors, and red velvet draperies.

I faced nine judges, also known as justices.

I was nervous at first, but I spoke out strongly for equal rights.

Would these stern men agree with my argument?

At that time, no woman had ever served on the United States Supreme Court.

Adding a female justice would be a good idea, don't you think?

MY LUCKY JEWELRY

For my first appearance at the Supreme Court in 1973, I wore my mother's gold earrings and her matching pin. I wanted to honor the woman who taught me that I could be as smart and as strong as any man. I also wanted to look good for my big day in court!

We won! Sharron was thrilled, and so was I.

I couldn't wait to take more cases to the Supreme Court.

I spent the next few years helping teachers, teenagers, pregnant women, single fathers, and many others seeking justice.

Most of the time, I won.

But there was still so much work to do.

To help women succeed in the workplace, I let my staff take care of their children on the job.

People weren't used to seeing toys and baby bottles in a law office!

RIGHTS FOR YOU, RIGHTS FOR ME

I became known as a champion of women's rights, but I believed just as strongly in rights for men. I hoped Jane and James could grow up in a country where all are equal under the law. They hoped so, too!

How could I make even more of a difference?

In 1980, I became a judge.

And then, in 1993, the president of the United States chose me to be one of the nine Supreme Court justices.

Can you believe a small, quiet, left-handed Jewish girl from Brooklyn would be the second female justice?

This was my best chance to defend the values dearest to my heart:

Equality and justice!

The Supreme Court's black robes were designed for men to wear with neckties.

When I joined, I added my own touch!

MY BIGGEST FAN

Before taking my place on the Supreme Court, I had to be approved by the United States Senate. My whole family joined me for this serious meeting, including my grandson, Paul. When I introduced them, I shared a book Paul had made called *My Grandma Is Very Special*. It made me laugh—and the senators, too!

On the Supreme Court, I stood up for ordinary folks.

Immigrants.

People of color.

Same-sex couples.

One of my greatest victories was helping women enter a male-only military school.

I was so proud when one of the new students rose to the top of her class.

Just as I once had!

The Supreme Court was yet another place with no women's restroom.

When I came on board, that changed once and for all!

"I DISSENT"

I did not always agree with the final Supreme Court decision. When I disagreed with the other justices, I could read a statement called a dissent. I became famous for strong dissents when I thought the court did not properly defend equal rights. It was necessary to show the country a different point of view—and I always wore a special rhinestone collar for the occasion!

Remember how my mother taught me to win an argument by showing respect?

That lesson served me well on the Supreme Court.

I tried to get along with every justice, even those who disagreed with me.

That way, we could politely share ideas.

Sometimes they changed my mind, and sometimes I changed theirs.

Justice Scalia and I were invited to appear in an opera.

I was not allowed to sing, of course, but at least I got to come onstage in a fancy wig!

THE ODD COUPLE

I became best friends with my fellow justice Antonin Scalia, even though we had very different views. I liked his sense of humor, and he liked mine. I loved music, and so did he. Antonin and I showed the world that two people can disagree about many things and still enjoy each other's company.

I never cared about being famous, but a funny thing happened when I got older.

I became a star!

People nicknamed me "RBG."

They put my name on T-shirts, coffee mugs, and posters.

They painted my face on their fingernails.

They even dressed up as me for Halloween.

It made me happy, because I knew what they were really celebrating . . .

I might not look strong . . .

. . . but I bet I can do more push-ups than you!

YOU'RE AS YOUNG AS YOU FEEL

I was glad to show the world that an older woman can be as powerful as anyone else. Along with my busy schedule at the Supreme Court, I went horseback riding, waterskiing, parasailing, and whitewater rafting. Not bad for a great-grandmother!

. . . They were celebrating the fight for fairness!

I led this fight for years, with many people by my side.

We came from different backgrounds but shared a single goal:

Equality and justice for all.

Won't you join us in making the world a better place?

As a girl, I dreamed of being just like my mother one day.

What kind of hero will you be when you grow up?

UNITED WE STAND

My favorite words come from the beginning of the Constitution: "We the People of the United States, in Order to form a more perfect Union . . ." This beautiful phrase inspires Americans to work together for the common good. If we try hard enough, we can make life better for one another!

AUTHOR'S NOTE

Young **Ruth Bader Ginsburg** (1933–2020) found a role model in her strong, caring mother. Celia Amster Bader lived at a time when women had few opportunities for an education or a career, but she taught Ruth to set big goals for herself. Though Celia died when Ruth was only 17, she remained a lifelong inspiration.

Growing up, Ruth experienced discrimination as a girl and as a member of the Jewish faith. But in college, she learned about the American values of justice and equality. She chose to fight for those ideals by becoming a lawyer.

Despite facing barriers for women at law school, Ruth succeeded with skill and determination. As a lawyer, she devoted herself to making the United States a fairer place. Throughout the 1970s, she helped men and women who suffered unequal treatment under the law. Though shy and quiet on the outside, she had the inner strength to achieve major legal victories.

Ruth's commitment to human rights led to her appointment as a Supreme Court justice in 1993. At her Supreme Court nomination ceremony, she honored her beloved mother. "I pray that I may be all that she would have been had she lived in an age when women could aspire and achieve," Ruth said.

Even those who disagreed with Justice Ginsburg respected her integrity and open-mindedness. She always searched for common ground with her opponents.

In old age, Ruth became an unlikely celebrity nicknamed "RBG." People fell in love with the tiny great-grandmother in oversize glasses and a lacy collar. They knew she had the heart of a lion, never tiring in her quest for justice and equality.

BE LIKE RUTH

- Learn to write well
- Read a lot
- Stand up for those less fortunate than you
- Be respectful even to those who disagree with you
- Follow your passions
- Have a great sense of humor

RBG STYLE

- Oversize glasses
- Hair pulled into a ponytail with a scrunchie
- A black robe with fancy collars for every occasion
- A "Super Diva" T-shirt for workouts
- Large wigs for opera appearances
- A Brooklyn accent, pronouncing *a*'s and *o*'s like "aww"

RESOURCES

- Carmon, Irin, and Shana Knizhnik. *Notorious RBG: The Life and Times of Ruth Bader Ginsburg.* New York: Dey St., 2015.
- De Hart, Jane Sherron. *Ruth Bader Ginsburg: A Life.* New York: Alfred A. Knopf, 2018.
- Demuth, Patricia Brennan, illustrated by Jake Murray. *Who Was Ruth Bader Ginsburg?* New York: Penguin Workshop, 2019.
- Ginsburg, Ruth Bader. *Ruth Bader Ginsburg: In Her Own Words.* Helena Hunt, editor. Chicago: Agate B2, 2018.
- Leder, Mimi, director. *On the Basis of Sex.* Focus Features movie, 2018.
- Levy, Debbie, illustrated by Elizabeth Baddeley. *I Dissent: Ruth Bader Ginsburg Makes Her Mark.* New York: Simon & Schuster Books for Young Readers, 2016.
- *Oyez*, website devoted to Supreme Court news and history. https://www.oyez.org/.
- West, Betsy, and Julie Cohen, directors. *RBG.* Magnolia Pictures International documentary, 2018.

ACKNOWLEDGMENTS

- Thanks to Katie Heit, Ken Geist, and Marietta Zacker for their guidance. —Dean Robbins

RUTH'S FABULOUS LIFE

March 15, 1933—Ruth Bader born in Brooklyn, New York; nicknamed "Kiki" as a baby because she kicked so much.

1937—Begins attending Jewish summer camp, where she learns to care for those less fortunate.

1950—Enters Cornell University; falls in love with both Constitutional law and fellow student Marty Ginsburg, whom she later marries.

1956—Enrolls in Harvard Law School, where she is one of only nine women in a class of more than 500.

1963—Becomes a professor at Rutgers Law School, where she fights for equal pay for women faculty members.

1972—Founds the Women's Rights Project to help poor women, women of color, immigrant women, and others facing inequality under the law.

1973—Argues her first case in front of the Supreme Court to end sex discrimination, and wins.

1980—Appointed as a judge on the US Court of Appeals by President Jimmy Carter and develops a reputation for fairness.

1993—Nominated to the United States Supreme Court by President Bill Clinton, becoming the first Jewish female justice; Marty holds the Bible for her swearing-in ceremony.

September 18, 2020—Dies at age 87 and becomes the first woman to lie in state (have her casket ceremonially presented) in the US Capitol.

IMPORTANT TERMS

Argument: A lawyer's statement in court to make a point about the law.

Constitution: The main set of laws for the United States.

Court: A place where lawyers and judges discuss issues related to the law.

Discrimination: Treating people unfairly for being part of a certain group.

Dissent: A judge's statement expressing disagreement with the court's official decision.

Equality: People having the same rights and opportunities no matter what they look like, where they come from, or what they believe.

Judge: A person who decides on important issues in a court.

Justice: Fair treatment. (Also another name for a judge.)

Law: The rules that people agree to follow.

Lawyer: Someone who uses knowledge of the law to help people.

Rights: Freedoms that are guaranteed by the government.

Senate: A part of the United States government in which people called senators help make laws.

Supreme Court: The highest court in the United States, where nine judges (called justices) make decisions about important issues.